fearless fernie

fearless fernie

Hanging Out With Fernie and Me

Poems by GARY SOTO
illustrated by REGAN DUNNICK

G. P. Putnam's Sons

Text copyright © 2002 by Gary Soto

Illustrations copyright © 2002 by Regan Dunnick

G. P. Putnam's Sons, Reg. U.S. Pat. & Tm. Off.
Published simultaneously in Canada.
Printed in the United States of America.
Book designed by Gunta Alexander.
Text set in Quorum Medium.

Library of Congress Cataloging-in-Publication Data
Soto, Gary. Fearless Fernie : hanging out with Fernie and me /
poems by Gary Soto ; illustrated by Regan Dunnick.   p. cm.
1. Children's poetry, American. [1. Best friends—Poetry.
2. Friendship—Poetry. 3. American poetry.] I. Dunnick, Regan, ill.
PS3569.O72 F4 2002   811'.54—dc21   2001019712
ISBN 0-399-23615-5
10 9 8 7

To Fernando Hernandez, a Fresno friend —G. S.

To my family —R. D.

Contents

Upstarts

In the first place
There was Mom and Dad, and Dad's mom and dad,
Then Mom's mom and dad,
Then music from a boom box,
Then sparks off a skateboard at midnight,
Then the second tier of an ice cream cone hitting the sidewalk.

That's what woke us, Fernie and me,
The sounds of the world, and pairs and pairs of grown-up eyes
Looking at us.

Sure, Fernie was in his house,
And me, I was in my house. But we were already buds,
Already meant to pluck grass and stuff it in our mouths.
We were born. We were here,
Both as bald as plucked chickens and clucking like chickens,
For neither of us knew a word.

Me, I pushed away Grandpa's carrot-thick finger.
Fernie, I know, spit out his mush.
We made our escape.
We crawled across rugs, each of us pulling our weight,
And made our way across lawns and patches of mud,
Through weeds tall as Zulu spears.

First sight.
Fernie was eating an apple that fell from a tree.
Me, I was sucking a stalk of grass.
Fernie! I called. It's Me!

Fernie crawled toward me, and I toward him—
We began to wrestle and pull each other's hair,
And, oh, how I squealed when he wrung my ears like washrags.

We were such good friends.

How Coach Told Me I Didn't Make the Cut

So Coach said, "Go out for a pass,"
And me, I took off, running hard
Because here was my one chance.

Coach yelled, "Farther! Farther!"
His arm cocked and ready to throw the football.

My legs were like pinwheels, a blur.
I ran with my hands out,
My fingers wiggling for the touch
Of a ball. Once it was in my arms,
I wouldn't fumble.
No, I would carry it in for a touchdown.

"Deeper, deeper," I heard him yell.
I outpaced a barking dog and an old man
On a rusty bicycle.
Coach got smaller and smaller,
Until he was just a fleck of dust on my eyelids.

I slowed down, caught my breath,
And rubbed my eyes. Was that Coach so far away?

I walked home. The living room was empty.
When I turned on the TV, crowds were cheering
Those who had made the team.

Questions for the New Teacher

So Fernie thought, I'll ask questions,
Lots of them, so the new teacher will think I'm smart,
You know, like Belinda over by the window,
Or Ricardo, that boy with his pants all the way
To his throat. Yeah, I'll ask and ask,
And the new teacher, from a little town I hear,
Will think I'm smart. My arm will be a spear
Going up and down, up and down. I'll ask,
How come the moon can't swallow the stars,
Big ole moon that's like a wide-open mouth.
That will get the new teacher thinking.
Maybe she don't know about the moon and the stars,
But I do because I once slept on our roof
One summer, and it was cold, cold up there.
You see, once the hot roof cools, the asphalt shingles
Get wet from dew. Luckily, I had a sleeping bag,
And my cat Corky was warm. Yeah, I'm going to ask,
Teacher, do you know what it feels like to roll
From the roof and crash on the ground?

I bet she don't know the answer to that one.

King Kong Versus Me

Me, I took a step. King Kong took a step.
I took another step, and King Kong took another step.

My eyes brimmed with fire,
Smoke billowing from my nose.

I took a giant step, and King Kong took another step.
I took an even bigger step, and the hairy guy took one, too.

I balled up my fist.
Sweat filled the lines on my palms.
I was mad! I could have torn down a bamboo forest
With one whack
Of my arm.

But we never hurled ourselves at each other and wrestled.
All of his steps were forward and mine, smart me,
Were backward.

Guilt

Fernie lay in bed, thinking of the past.
He remembered his friends from third grade—
Hector, Michael, Liz, Liz's big brother, Mark,
And Mark's two friends.

Fernie paraded around the school with his friends.
They lived off each other's happiness.
What was better than getting wet when the sprinklers came on!
What was tastier than the juice from their Popsicles
They licked from their wrists!

Then Fernie remembered the boy
With no friends, the boy

Who during recess
Took his lunch into the far corner
And ate. He had no one but the sparrows that had dropped
From the tree. The boy ate his dry sandwich.

Fernie thought of the boy.
Was he still there, in the far corner of the playground?
Were the sparrows there, or did they fly elsewhere
Once the boy—what's his name—had nothing to give,
His lunch all gone, loneliness like crumbs at his feet.

Body Parts in Rebellion

The fist bragged that he guarded me at school.
The legs said, "We keep you going."

The tongue, a small carpet, rolled and rolled
In its moist cave. The teeth yelled,
"Don't throw stones at the crowd that cheers you!"

The eyes said, "We're the ones that lead the way."
The belly moaned, "I will suffer the most!"
The nose sniffed. The ears picked up the sound
Of an ice cream truck.

They conspired while I sat at the dinner table,
Sneering at nine Brussels sprouts.

"Don't do it!" the right hand screamed.
"I'll slap you," the palm warned.
"You want me to gag?" the throat whined.
None of my body parts wanted anything to do
With the veggies now cold on the plate.

The moon came up.
The stars rotated in the cold, cold sky.
I sat at the dining table, my body in rebellion,
Juggling the Brussels sprouts when my parents went off to bed.

Medicine

Fernie heard Laughter is a medicine,
But cried when he struck
His thumb with a bat,

All because he was hanging a picture of himself
On the wall. He used a bat,

Not a hammer,
Which hung in the garage.

He was too lazy to go out there.

His thumb went into his mouth
And then out of his mouth.

He laughed.
He laughed at his thumb.
He laughed at the picture of himself laughing.
He tickled himself for more pleasure.

The phone rang in the hallway.
When he answered, it was his best friend, me.
I asked Fernie, "What are you doing?"

"Just laughing," he sobbed, petting his red rooster of a thumb.
"Just having a good time."

Dance Lessons

Fernie said to the broom, "May I have this dance?"
He took the broom into his arms
And swung it left and right,
Dipped it,
Balanced in the center of his palm
This broom suddenly called Rebecca.

He waltzed Rebecca into the kitchen
And back into the living room,
Dust and dust mites stirring from the floor.
He cooed, "Rebecca, my broom, I mean my love,
You have a nice personality."

He did the cha-cha, a samba, a cumbia, a tango.
Thirsty, he drank a glass of water
And offered a sip to his broom, I mean his love,
But she had no mouth.

Fernie made conversation. Fernie said,
"The vacuum cleaner is a monster of hoses and attachments."
Tears bloomed in his eyes. He whispered tenderly how he preferred
Brooms to people and of all brooms, the one in his arms.
He said, "I like to eat and baseball is my favorite sport."
He would have spoken louder and longer, but she had no ears.
He plucked a straw from her skirt and Rebecca didn't scream.

But Fernie's sister screamed when she came into the house.
"I gotta go somewhere real quick!"

She pushed Fernie aside
And flew away on his first dance partner, the broom called Rebecca.

Fall Football

Autumn swung down from the tree,
Leaf by leaf.

Me, I put away my baseball glove.
I picked up the football

And ran after a pass I tossed in the air,
Not far but far enough to make me a hero—
I tripped myself to build up grass stains on my knees
And rolled on the lawn
While my cat, the one fan, watched from the sidelines.

The score remained 7–0, then went up to 14–0.
The game ended when the first porch light on the block
    snapped on.

The interview from the press followed:
"Me, tell me about the game."

I wiped my forehead. I massaged my shoulder,
Sore from all the passes I had to catch on my own.

"It was a personal challenge," I said, exhausted.
"It's always hard when I play against myself."

Stealing

Hands like two crabs in boiling water
When Mom finds out.

What Fernie Thought

When Fernie was five and school was over for the day,
He thought his teacher, Miss Alexander, went into the closet,
Stood there among the brooms
And maybe a stringy mop.

Maybe Miss Alexander stood with one foot in a pail.
Maybe she clapped the erasers for fun.

Fernie worried over dinner about his teacher.
She had no water or food, except a little bit in her stomach.
If she wanted to exercise, she could turn in a circle.

Where did his teacher go at night? The closet.
That's why Miss Alexander, thin as a mop,
Clapped two erasers and cried, "Oh, it's so good to see you!"
When the first children arrived at school.

Spelling Bee

So the judge with bird's nests for eyebrows
Said, "Fernie, spell 'egg.' "
Fernie wet his lips, whistled, and looked out on the audience,
All of whom had had eggs for breakfast.
His own stomach contained an egg
And his head, they said, was shaped like an egg
When he was first born.

"Egg," the judge called,
His bird's nests going up and down. "The word is 'egg.' "

Fernie licked his lips.
He liked Easter and he liked eggs,
All dyed and hidden in the grass and high weeds.
He liked eggs with pancakes, which were also made of eggs.

His mother squeezed her Kleenex.
She was a worried mom.

"Thirty more seconds," the judge called.
The audience hushed. Though three in the front row
Were cracking hard-boiled eggs against their chairs.

"Egg," Fernie started. "E-G-G."
The audience applauded.
His mother sighed and wiped her brow.

Then the judge smoothed his bird's nests
And turned to me. "Spell 'ball.' "

Me, I always get the hard ones.

Fishing

Me, I fit a marble-sized gob of bread on a hook
And threw the line into the river.

Clouds passed, raining three crows
Who pecked at my feet, curious at my pastime,

For I was a boy and most boys were wrestling on lawns.
The crows flew away. About noon,

The sun flattened the grass from its enormous heat.
Oh, I was hot but I was fishing,

Bored out of my mind until the line began to tug.
I tugged, and the "thing" under the water tugged.

We went back and forth, and I was sure it was a whale,
No, a mermaid, no, an octopus with one red ugly eye.

But when the "thing" stopped to rest, I fit a sandwich
Into my mouth. I needed to stoke my belly.

The crows returned, for I had to pull with all my strength.
It was me against nature, I thought,

And I yanked, pulled, and tugged
Until the "thing" came up, wet Fernie sleek as a dolphin.

"Fernie!" I yelled. "So that's where you were!"

Third-Grade Genius

Me, I took two wires, a battery, and a bulb
And fit them nicely together in my hand.

Show and tell.

I said, "I know about electricity."
Then I walked up and down the aisles, showing my invention,
A flashlight of sorts. This on a rainy day,
With the battery of the sun gone dead.
This on a day when the headlights of cars came on at noon.

Me, I showed my friends about electricity,
The beam of my invention glinting off the teacher's glasses.
I beamed it at the hamster, whose eyes glowed red as berries.

I sat down, a magician who brought light to the classroom.
I kicked my legs, ropes hanging from the chair.
I was happy.

School ended.
The rain started to throw darts on our shoulders.
But I didn't worry. I had a baseball cap
And my invention in my hand,
The one-eyed headlight that brightened the sidewalk
On the way back home.

Our Substitute Teacher Named Abraham

Our substitute teacher, a guy with a long ponytail,
Said that we should make art, crazy art.
He said, "Don't draw what you see but what you feel!"
He touched his heart, then smoothed the rope of his ponytail.
"Don't draw a face but the egg of a face, the pancake of a face,
The starfish of a face. Yeah, don't draw a hand,
But the root of a hand, the pliers of a hand,
The bent fork of a hand!"

Me, I didn't know what he wanted.
I raised my hand.

"Yes, the spear of an arm,
The telephone of an arm, the lost broom of an arm!" he cried.

The class brought out its pencils.
Me, I licked mine and started to draw my best friend, Fernie,
While the substitute teacher leaned against the table,
Playing with his ponytail.

After fifteen minutes, the substitute teacher
Walked up and down the aisles.

He stopped at my desk. I thought I was in trouble,

But he clapped his hands. "Oh, yes," he screamed at my Fernie
    picture.
"The wet cat of a storm, the feathers of a storm,
The fence of a storm!"

"Is it good?" I asked.
"No, it's better than great!" he yelled happily.
"It's the peach of great, the apple of great, the strawberry of great!"
I felt proud of my drawing!

When the bell then rang for recess, all of us stormed
From the class, me screaming, "The home run of a boy,
The goal of a boy, the touchdown of a boy!"

Confidence

Fernie joined the track team
And heard on the first day, Long legs is what gets you going.

He looked at his legs, short as a short dog's hind legs.

At home, he had two friends swing him around by his ankles,
But when they let go, he flew into the air,
His fall cushioned by a bush.

His legs were still short.

Day of the race,
He walked in the sun,
And his shadow cast legs long as the hand on a sundial.
He wiggled a foot, then another foot,
Each long as canoes.

But in the starter's block, his body bunched up,
His legs shrunk. When the gun sounded, the crowd roared,
The runners leaped like fleas.

Fernie crawled out, like a roly-poly bug,
His hundred tiny legs churning, but how slow!

Orange Socks

Me, I blame the washer for eating all my socks,
The black pair, the blue pair, the green pair.

Then the fall dance arrived.
I put on my fuzzy orange socks.
I put on my black pants, white shirt, black shoes,
Their tips shining like mirrors.

At the dance, the girls ran away.
The bad boys laughed and spit ice cubes at me.
The teachers took up a collection to buy me dark socks.

Me, I hung out near the window,
Talking to myself.

The lights went out.
The boys screamed and slipped on the ice cubes they spat at me.
The girls dropped their purses. The coins the teachers
Had collected rolled away,
Down the steps and into the street.

"Don't panic," I ordered. "Hold on to me."
A girl hooked her hands on my waist, and a boy hooked his
    hands onto her.
We became a human chain, me the hero as I led them out
By the glow of my orange socks.

Fernie's Batting Average

It was a check swing on an oh-and-two count,
But the ball flew over center field,
Over the fence and over the parking lot.
The ball picked up speed—
Sailed over the telephone wire and Denny's,
Nearly hitting a blimp before it fell earthward hot as coal.

The ball landed sizzling in a cow patch
And started the grass on fire—
Herd of three thousand cows running crazily
From the tumbleweed of smoke.

And that was only the first inning.

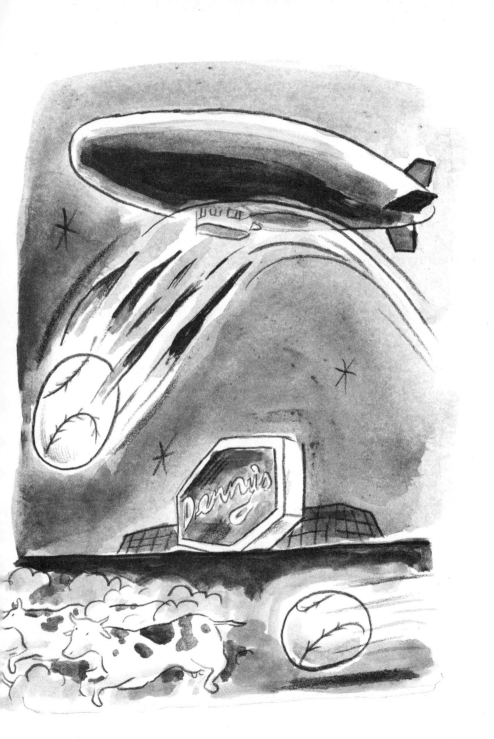

Fearless Fernie

Fernie put on muscle,
Big plates on his chest, ropes in his arms,
Trout shimmering under the skin
Of his brown shoulders.
His waist was thin as an ant's.

And me? Heck, I sat on the lawn eating potato chips,
This after two hot dogs and a can of bean dip,
Plus a fistful of black jelly beans.
It hurt me to watch Fernie lifting weights in the garage.
His face was purple and his eyes nearly popped out
When he hoisted the tonnage of two beat-up cars.

He stood up, breathing hard.
He leaned against the door and yelled, "Ow!"
A wooden sliver with the weight of an eyelash punctured his skin.

Big baby, he pushed his thumb into his mouth.

Itching the Itch, or How to Get a Soda

My sister said, "Scratch my back."
I took a Popsicle stick and scratched slowly.

"Faster," she yelled.
I scratched even slower.

"Come on!" she yelled.
The scratching came slower,
The speed of a potato bug walking on a sidewalk.

She pushed me away and dropped to the floor,
Scrubbing her back like a dog.

Then our dog, confused, lay on his back and scratched.
I lay down, too, and wiggled on the ground,
All three of us barking.

Then Mom came into the living room, hands on her hips.
"Okay. Cold sodas for your act!"

Bad Mood

Why lift weights
When I have to lug my math book, a boulder in my arms.

Why wash the car
When bugs keep flying into the windshield.

Why wake up
When every night I jump back in at a quarter to ten.

Why be nice
When your friends still talk behind your back.

Why do anything!
Let the dishes pile in the sink
And the lawn grow into a hedge.
I'm in a bad mood. I'm going to roll
Onto the grass
And onto my belly.
One ear to the ground, I can hear the earth grumbling, too.

Rumor

You know the girl in the third row?
She's like an apple—sweet on the outside
But bitter at the core.

Cannibal Sandwich

Two pieces of bread, ham, a slice of poor cheese with holes,
And a layer of potato chips. Slap the ham silly with mustard!

Close the sandwich.

When you bite down, the chips shatter like bones.

Big Eaters

I stepped into the cold rush
Of a river until I was waist deep.
I screamed, "Check out this twenty-foot trout,"
But the people on the shore
Kept eating their hot dogs and hamburgers.
I called, "There's a mermaid down here!"
But they only pushed their hands into bags
Of potato chips and sucked on ice.
I shouted, "Hey, a shark almost bit my toes!"
They lapped their ice creams
And bit into cookies.

No one seemed excited.
When I stepped out of the water
And looked at the sandy shore,
I called, "Hey, the steaks are almost done!"

Everyone came running with their forks.

Emotions

For sadness, Fernie pondered the three holes in his socks.
For happiness, he fit a pair of wax lips on his mouth.

For loneliness, he swallowed a cloud.
For excitement, he made the spring from a pen leap like a flea.

Fernie wrote his thoughts on the back of an envelope.
He was getting to know himself. He wrote, I'm five feet tall.
Weigh 102 pounds. I once tortured a daisy
By pulling off its petals.

For boredom, he shuffled a deck of cards and played solitaire.
For greed, he licked a candy bar wrapper.

Fernie, our sixth-grade hero, was in trouble with his mother,
All because for fun he polished the dining room table with car wax.

Now he was grounded. He sat in a chair in his bedroom,
A rat in the corner and shadows on the walls
Where bred fear, the largest of all emotions,
Fear that his mother would say, "Okay, that's enough,"

And she would force him to come out.

On the Escalator at Macy's

Me, I try to be nice,
But one day on the escalator,
A grumpy woman snarled at me,
All because my shoelaces were undone,
Or maybe it was the hole in my T-shirt—
My belly button poked out like an eyeball.

I smiled, she snarled.
I smiled even bigger, and she hissed like a snake.
I remembered to be nice and said, "What are you going to buy
    today?"
Her mouth snapped shut
And her fiery eyes poked another hole in my T-shirt.

She muttered, "I'm glad I don't have kids!"
That's what grumpy people say to the world.

When we got off the escalator,
I took her with me, her face in my memory,
Ah, her grumpy mouth snapping like a mousetrap,
And kids like me, mouselike, trying to wiggle out of her bite.

My Name on the Kitchen Window

I cloud my breath on the window
And write my name backwards.
This is my mark.
Which slowly weeps down the glass.
It's just like me. I'm sad about something I can't name.
Maybe it's my clothes, or perhaps my shoes—
Rat-brown, I hide them under my bed when they're not on my
    feet.

I breathe on the window and write my name.
Birds fly past. The kite on the telephone wire wags its tail.
The gardener takes down his mower from the back of his truck.
These are the small activities on a small street.

I scrub the glass with my sleeve, then inhale deeply.
I have to breathe on the window for my name to reappear.

Who's Calling?

I carved my name on a tree trunk,
Then added my phone number.

This was last spring. Now it's the end of summer,
And my family has a new number. Maybe this happened:
Some girl was swinging from a limb
When she saw my name and number.
With a finger, she traced them over and over,
Like the blind reading braille.

She ran home, called, and heard the recorded voice:
"The number you have called is no longer in service."
This girl, I like to think, was in the tree
Because she was lonely, perhaps unwanted.
She had to talk to someone, even me.

What are trees but telephone books,
Carved with names and numbers, plus hearts,
All hurting from the arrows that stick through them.

Description of the Suspect

Once, during trick-or-treat,
Fernie saw an older boy tear a bag of candy
From a small boy and run
Down the street, candies spilling.
Since he was as tall as that thief,
He took after that boy. He yelled, "Stop him! Stop him!"
When he looked back, he saw
Others running . . . after him!
He thought, No, I'm not the thief.
He's the one!

The thief got away, but Fernie saw him:
He wore a dark jacket, white shoes,
And sported an earring in his left
Ear . . . just like him! A chill
Spread across his shoulders.
Fernie was like that boy, only different.

Birthday Party for Fernie and Me

Me, I made the cake and waited
To sing "Happy Birthday" at the top of my lungs,
To spank myself twelve times, my age,
To blow out the finger-length candles,
To shout, "For me!"

I cut a slice of cake,
The mud of sweetness cleared away with a glass of milk.

I washed my plate and glass, plus the fork,
Popped a red balloon, and said, "That was fun!"
Then Fernie showed up. "Sorry, but I had to cut the lawn.
Now cut me some cake."

I unwrapped my present from Fernie.
I stared at an inflatable globe,
Large as a basketball when I got my lungs going.

Then Fernie and me sat in the living room,
Rolling the inflated globe between us,
Neither of us wanting any part of the world's problems.

I tossed it at his face, and he tossed it at mine,
Both of us leaking tears on my birthday. It's not funny
When big old Australia hits you square in the eye!

Bodyguard

When I joined the track team,
Fernie said, "You need a bodyguard to protect your knees."

I ignored my friend, who now shadowed me,
Who went everywhere I went. When I put a cereal spoon
Into my mouth, Fernie pulled it out, examined it.
"Just checking for germs."

Fernie carried my books, he opened doors for me.
He held my feet when I did sit-ups
And tossed me a clean towel when I finished my push-ups.

Truth is, Fernie was always in my way!
When I read a page or two in science,
He cooled my eyes with wet paper towels—
"You don't want to ruin your eyes!" he said.

One day at lunchtime, Fernie fought a fight for me.
He got his nose bloody, he scuffed his fists on a boy's chin.
He even stayed after school when the principal found out!

On the day of the race, I slipped into my shoes,
Weightless as shaving cream,
And walked out to the track.

Teachers and friends cheered. Even a sparrow chirped
When I got into the starting block.
But when the starter's gun popped,
Fernie jumped onto my back.

"What are you doing?" I asked.
"Protecting you," he answered.

Me, I staggered with my best friend on my back,
Staggered over the flat sandy ground.
When I looked back, I saw my footprints,
Huge dents in the track.

Midway through the race, I was slowly sinking into the sand.
Fernie was now standing on my shoulders,
My bodyguard looking around for trouble.
Eyeing the finish line—last place but not one scratch on me!

Fernie and Me Go Camping

"Man, I'd hate to lose the key to the cabin in this snow," I said,
But six steps into our walk to the river I was patting my four
  pockets.
Fernie patted his two pockets and screamed, "Oh, no!"
He next patted mine and I patted his, then we wrestled like bears
And blamed the other, the darn snow,
And finally society for our upbringing.

Afterward Fernie sat on a granite rock, tall as a moose.
He said, "This rock has been here longer than air or fire.
And bronze and iron are but babes to this rock. Aluminum
Was born yesterday." It was something to say.

I said to Fernie, "I always liked snow,"
And rubbed handfuls on my left cheek.
When my smile didn't bring a smile to his face
I stopped talking. I popped a knuckle. I was twelve, already lost.
Poor us, I thought, we can't get into the cabin,
Where there's hot chocolate and a roll of Life Savers.
We looked into the window—our beds were waiting for us.

I snapped my fingers. "I know," I screamed.
"When an airplane flies by, we should raise our faces to the sky."

I explained how the sun would gleam off our tears,
Salty as the sea. We would move our jaws, moving slightly,
Then vigorously, the Morse code of boyish stupidity.

What They Don't Tell You About Cereal

In love, Fernie ate three bowls of cereal,
The flakes coated with sugar.
He put down his spoon and flew around the house.
There was rocket fuel in his heart.

Then he sat down to write a love note to Marta,
A girl in the second row, you know, by the window?
Marta, he wrote, I have a secret:
I LOVE YOU! I LOVE YOU! I LOVE YOU!

When his rocket fuel burned off,
He poured another bowl so that he could finish his note.
Again, he flew around the house,
Then sat down to write: I DO! I DO! I DO!

By the end of this note, all the cereal was gone.
His fingers were blistered from holding the pencil,
Sharpened so many times it was a nub
When he finally signed his name: FERNIE, FERNIE, FERNIE.

What Fernie Learned

Fernie was walking along the street,
Eating the sweet guts of a watermelon.
He spit out the seeds,
Let the juice of the melon run down his arm.

Then he stopped and his hair jumped on his head.
He saw a quarter embedded in the asphalt.
It was his lucky day!

On his knees, in the wind of the oncoming cars,
He dug with his fingernails
For that quarter,
He dug until his fingertips were bleeding
But he thought, I could buy candy with that money.

Sweat was pouring from his brow
When the quarter came loose. He was breathing hard.
His knees were grimy from the road.
When he looked back at his watermelon on the curb,
He discovered a whole nation of black ants
Feasting on the rind.
One brave ant was even carrying a seed away.

When you leave something sweet behind,
Others come and get it.

Fernie and Me Try Art

Fernie said, "Let's try painting,"
And, massaging my chin, I said, "It's okay by me."

But Fernie said, "But I don't want you to steal my ideas."
And me, I said, "Man, I don't want you to steal my ideas, either!"

I went home and painted the sunset on the back of my eyelids
After I stared into a flashlight.

I drew happy faces on the tips of my fingertips—
A family of five drowning in the soapy water of the kitchen sink.

I drew a cow on paper, then changed the cow into an elephant
By adding a nose. I massaged my chin. Ah, what genius!

I painted the sky on my ceiling, and colored a boiled egg.
I answered the telephone: "Yes, it's me, the artist."

I grew confident. I took my creations to Fernie's place.
I called, "Hey, Fernie Picasso, where are you?"

Fernie was dressed in his bathing suit,
A bucket of paint in one hand and
A dripping roller in the other.
"What are you doing?" I asked.

He raised the dripping roller to the garage.
"Painting the window," Fernie answered.

And I wanted to say, That's not painting!
But Fernie was my friend. So I said,
"Trim on windows is really hard to do, huh?"

Not knowing what else to say, I pressed my face to the window
And came away with my eyelashes blinking white.

Art Collectors

Me, I became an artist on the weekend.
I took my markers out in the field
And drew what I saw:
Two ants were carrying a twig
Three times their size, no, a lot bigger,
Something like a telephone pole.

Then I slept in the field.
When I woke, the two ants were carrying away
My artwork, a sheet of paper that was like a sail
On their heads. How they got it into their hole
And onto their wall—millions of ants coming by
To admire my art—I don't know.

Palm Reading

Me: My line leads to the store for donuts.
Fernie: No, mine brings me to an oily river.

Me: This line leads to Great America.
Fernie: No, a dark alley of cats with bent whiskers.

Me: The bend in this line says I'm going to find a sock of money.
Fernie: Yes, a sock with a rat living inside.

Me: This line leads to a three-sports career.
Fernie: Nah, a chair in a dark hospital overrun with spiders.

We became quiet
As we sat on the lawn, me convinced of the future
And Fernie moody as a toad.

"What's wrong?" I asked.

Fernie pushed a stalk of grass into his mouth,
Poor Fernie, who earlier had dropped ten pop-ups
While his family was watching. His team, the Lucky Stars,
Lost 13–3.

"I don't know," he said,
Spanking his palm that should have caught
The pop-ups. "I wish I had your hands."

At the River Called Sadness

Me, I should have floated off like a log.
You see, I whispered this girl's name
Over and over
And heard what the owl said,
My big-eyed companion in the cottonwood—
Who? Who? Who?

I scratched the sand with my fingers.
I wrote her name with a stick
And patted fool's gold into the lines
Of my palms.

You see, this was the first girl I liked.
But she shrugged her shoulders and said, *"Who?"*
When she heard my name at school.

I could have jumped into the river, I felt so sad.
I talked to the dirty faces
Of my fingertips.
I said, "She doesn't even know me!"

The sun wheeled over my head.
Rivers carried snowmelt
And fish, and they carried boys,
Heavy as logs, who piled up downstream
When girls, like owls, said, *"Who? Who?"*

Close Your Eyes and Make a Wish

For my tenth birthday,
Me, I put eleven candles into the cake, looking to the future.
Fernie said, "Why not twelve?"

"Not a bad idea, amigo," I told Fernie.
I put in three more candles.

"You're not fourteen!" Fernie shouted,
His fork in the air because he was ready to grub!

I agreed. Still, I closed my eyes
And felt the warmth of the lit candles.
I saw orange behind my eyelids.
I saw my chin with its first little whiskers.
I saw myself with chest muscles big as hubcaps
And a brick in each arm.
Boy, was I strong!

I dreamed behind my closed eyes.
My face became warmer
And the orange behind my closed eyes grew oranger.
I saw myself at sixteen and a girl cooing, "You're so brave!"
This after I tamed a shark that wouldn't behave.
Poor guy, I had to punch him in his big old snout
And send him back into the deep sea.

More danger on the beach!
I had to tie a nasty octopus into a tangle of shoelaces
And save surfers drowning two feet from the shore.
Boy, was I strong!

My face became really hot. I opened my eyes.
Fernie had stuck a hundred candles into my cake.

"Fernie," I yelled, "my cake's on fire!"
The two of us blew out the candles,
And since we were more talk than action,
Boy, did we have a lot of breath inside us.

Then we licked the candles, each a smoky lighthouse.
Our forks, circling like seagulls,
Flew down and courageously rescued two
Little figures—Fernie and me—nearly drowning in a sugar sea.

Big Boy Courage

Fernie and me on the roof
And neither of us saying, We're buds for life.
But we are.

Fernie rolls a Life Saver off the pitched roof.
It falls silently, perhaps on the head of an unlucky ant.

I could ask, Fernie, how come you did that?
But I don't. He doesn't like orange-flavored Life Savers.

The sun goes down. The first stars freeze, then start rotating.
An airplane goes west, then banks east,
And Fernie and me can't make up our minds whether to jump
From the roof, or yell for help.

The moon is a white yawn.
We yawn, too. We eat Life Savers,
And then Fernie says, "You ready?"

I swallow a lozenge of fear
And gather up courage. My legs are like a wobbly chair.
"This is it," Fernie says.
We jump at the same time, arms out like wings.

A two-foot fall from a doghouse,
The dog greets our landing with his happy tongue.

Friends Forever

We lived our lives on the front lawn,
And it was time for Fernie and me to try a snowy mountain
    peak
Where we could speak to a mountain goat
And yodel to the valley below.

We put on our boots.
Then we took them off and put on plastic sandwich bags
Over our socks. We knew snow was cold and wet,
And we must be prepared.

We took a bus to the country, transferring two times—
All this traveling for a crisp dollar bill.
When we got out, our breath immediately hung in the air.
The air was fresh, the sky blue.

Me, I said, "O fresh air! O blue sky!"
Fernie nudged me: "Buddy, save it for up there."
"There" was a mountain steep as a ladder
But many times higher.

We climbed and climbed, then rested.
I pointed: "Hey, there's the bus!"
Me, I sang, "O bus that carried us this far!
O bus with plenty of nickels we found on the floor!"

Again, Fernie said, "Save it!"
We climbed and then fit gobs of snow into our mouths,
For we were thirsty. A mountain goat came up
And looked at us. The goat, too, lowered his face
And began to eat snow.

Thus, in our youth, we had influenced nature:
The goat ate, then two birds flew from a pine tree and ate.
Then a weasel, a raccoon, and a bobcat with his pointed ears,
All of us devouring the sumptuous white!

Then, wow, an elephant from nowhere arrived
To hose up his share of the snow.

We were blinking animals,
Yodeling our own language.
We were no longer thirsty.
We were happy.

I leaned on Fernie's shoulder, and the elephant leaned on me.
I finally sang, "O fresh air! O blue sky!
O bus that carried us this far!"
Friends forever in the wonderful snow.

WITHDRAWN